THE OXFORD PIANO METHOD

PIANO TIME CAROLS

19 really easy arrangements by

Pauline Hall

CONTENTS

This book belongs to _____

Address _____

Date _____

Away in a manger

W. J. Kirkpatrick (1838–1921)

1. A-way in a manger, no crib for a bed, The little Lord Jesus laid down his sweet head; The stars in the bright sky looked down where he lay, The little Lord Jesus a-sleep on the hay.

2 The cattle are lowing,
    The baby awakes,
  But little Lord Jesus
    No crying he makes.
  I love thee, Lord Jesus!
    Look down from the sky,
  And stay by my side until
    Morning is nigh.

3 Be near me, Lord Jesus;
    I ask thee to stay
  Close by me for ever,
    And love me, I pray.
  Bless all the dear children
    In thy tender care,
  And fit us for heaven,
    To live with thee there.

Anon.

Printed in Great Britain
OXFORD UNIVERSITY PRESS, MUSIC DEPARTMENT, GREAT CLARENDON STREET, OXFORD OX2 6DP

I saw three ships

English traditional carol

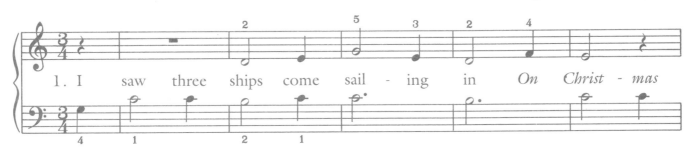

2 And what was in those ships all three?
   On Christmas Day, on Christmas Day,
   And what was in those ships all three?
   On Christmas Day in the morning.

3 Our Saviour Christ and his Lady.

4 Pray, whither sailed those ships all three?

5 O, they sailed into Bethlehem.

6 And all the bells on earth shall ring.

3

Kings of Orient

Optional accompaniment

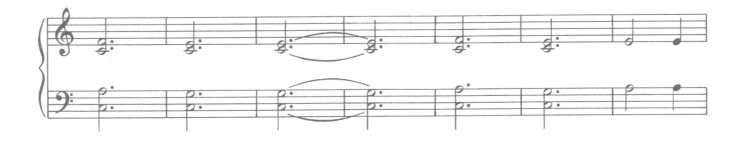

Kings of Orient

Words and melody by J. H. Hopkins (1820–91)

Solo*

We three kings of O - ri - ent are; Bear - ing gifts we
tra - verse a - far Field and foun - tain, moor and moun - tain,
Fol - low - ing yon - der star: O star of won - der,
star of night, Star with ro - yal beau - ty bright, West - ward
lead - ing, still pro - ceed - ing, Guide us to thy per - fect light.

*To be played 1 octave higher if accompaniment is used.

5

In dulci jubilo

German, 14th-century
tr. R. L. Pearsall (1795–1856)

Old German carol

In dul - ci ju - bi - lo[a] _____ Let us our ho - mage

shew; _____ Our heart's joy re - clin - eth In prae -

- se - pi - o[b] _____ And like a bright star shin -

- eth Ma - tris in gre - mi - o.[c] _____ Al - pha

es et O,[d] _____ Al - pha es et O! _____

[a] in tuneful joy   [b] in a stable   [c] on his mother's lap   [d] You are Alpha and Omega—the beginning and the end.

Good King Wenceslas

Melody from *Piae Cantiones* (1582)

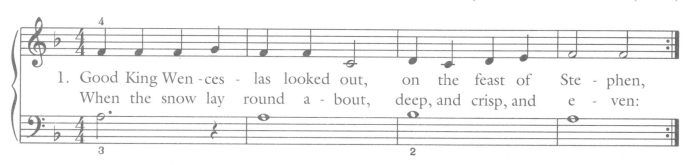

1. Good King Wen-ces-las looked out, on the feast of Ste-phen,
When the snow lay round a-bout, deep, and crisp, and e-ven:

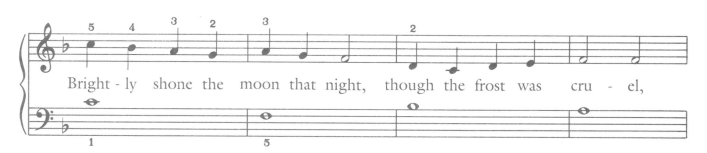

Bright-ly shone the moon that night, though the frost was cru-el,

When a poor man came in sight, gath'-ring win-ter fu - el.

2 'Hither, page, and stand by me,
　If thou know'st it, telling,
Yonder peasant, who is he?
　Where and what his dwelling?'
'Sire, he lives a good league hence,
　Underneath the mountain,
Right against the forest fence,
　By Saint Agnes' fountain.'

3 'Bring me flesh, and bring me wine,
　Bring me pine-logs hither:
Thou and I will see him dine,
　When we bear them thither.'
Page and monarch, forth they went,
　Forth they went together;
Through the rude wind's wild lament
　And the bitter weather.

4 'Sire, the night is darker now,
　And the wind blows stronger;
Fails my heart, I know not how;
　I can go no longer.'
'Mark my footsteps, good my page;
　Tread thou in them boldly:
Thou shalt find the winter's rage
　Freeze thy blood less coldly.'

5 In his master's steps he trod,
　Where the snow lay dinted;
Heat was in the very sod
　Which the saint had printed.
Therefore, Christian men, be sure,
　Wealth or rank possessing,
Ye who now will bless the poor,
　Shall yourselves find blessing.

J. M. Neale (1818–66)

7

O come, all ye faithful

Optional accompaniment

O come, all ye faithful

tr. F. Oakeley (1802–80) and others   Words and melody by J. F. Wade (*c.*1711-86)

Solo*

O come, all ye faith - ful, Joy - ful and tri - umph - ant, O

come ye, O come __ ye to Beth - le - hem;

Come and be - hold him Born the King of An - gels: O

come, let us a - dore him, O come, let us a - dore him, O

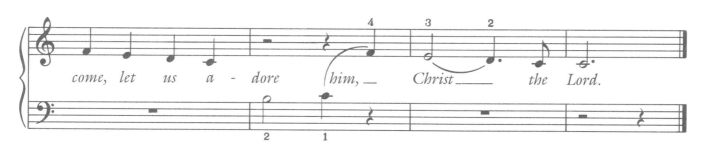

come, let us a - dore him, __ Christ ___ the Lord.

*To be played 1 octave higher if accompaniment is used.

9

While shepherds watched their flocks

'Winchester Old'

1. While shep-herds watched their flocks by night, All seat-ed on the

ground, The an-gel of the Lord came down, And glo-ry shone a-round.

2 'Fear not,' said he (for mighty dread
   Had seized their troubled mind);
   'Glad tidings of great joy I bring
   To you and all mankind.

3 'To you in David's town this day
   Is born of David's line
   A Saviour, who is Christ the Lord;
   And this shall be the sign:

4 'The heav'nly Babe you there shall find
   To human view displayed,
   All meanly wrapped in swathing bands,
   And in a manger laid.'

5 Thus spake the seraph; and forthwith
   Appeared a shining throng
   Of angels praising God, who thus
   Addressed their joyful song:

6 'All glory be to God on high,
   And to the earth be peace;
   Goodwill henceforth from heav'n to men
   Begin and never cease.'

N. Tate (1652–1715)

Deck the hall

Welsh traditional carol

Solo [Right hand only]

Deck the hall with boughs of hol - ly, *Fa la la la la, fa la la la,*

'Tis the sea - son to be jol - ly, *Fa la la la la, fa la la la.*

Fill the mead cup, drain the bar - rel, *Fa la la, fa la la, la la la,*

Troll the an - cient Christ - mas ca - rol, *Fa la la la la, fa la la la.*

Accompaniment

The first Nowell

Optional accompaniment

The first Nowell

Solo*

English traditional carol

The__ first__ No - well the__ an - gel did say Was to cer - tain poor shep - herds in fields as they lay; In__ fields__ where they lay,__ keep - ing their sheep, On a cold win - ter's night__ that was__ so deep: No - well, No - well, No - well, No - well, Born is the King__ of Is - ra - el!

*To be played 1 octave higher if accompaniment is used.

Silent night

Franz Gruber (1787–1863)

1. Silent night, holy night, All is calm, all is bright; Round yon virgin mother and child. Holy infant so tender and mild, Sleep in heavenly peace, Sleep in heavenly peace.

2 Silent night, holy night,
Shepherds first saw the sight:
Glories stream from heaven afar,
Heav'nly hosts sing Alleluia:
Christ the Saviour is born,
Christ the Saviour is born!

J. Mohr (1792–1848)

Once in royal David's city

H. J. Gauntlett (1805–76)

Solo [with optional accompaniment]

1. Once in ro-yal Da-vid's ci-ty stood a low-ly cat-tle_ shed,
Where a mo-ther laid_ her_ ba-by in a man-ger for_ his_ bed:

Ma-ry was that mo-ther mild, Je-sus Christ her lit-tle_ child.

Optional accompaniment

R.H.
L.H.

2 He came down to earth from heaven,
   Who is God and Lord of all,
  And his shelter was a stable,
   And his cradle was a stall;
  With the poor, and mean, and lowly,
   Lived on earth our Saviour holy.

3 And our eyes at last shall see him,
   Through his own redeeming love,
  For that child so dear and gentle
   Is our Lord in heav'n above;
  And he leads his children on
   To the place where he is gone.

C. F. Alexander (1818–95)

God rest you merry, gentlemen

Optional accompaniment

2 From God our heav'nly Father
       A blessed angel came,
   And unto certain shepherds
       Brought tidings of the same,
   How that in Bethlehem was born
       The Son of God by name:
           O tidings of comfort and joy,
               Comfort and joy,
           O tidings of comfort and joy.

3 Now to the Lord sing praises,
       All you within this place,
   And with true love and brotherhood
       Each other now embrace;
   This holy tide of Christmas
       All others doth deface:
           O tidings of comfort and joy,
               Comfort and joy,
           O tidings of comfort and joy.

God rest you merry, gentlemen

English traditional carol

Solo*

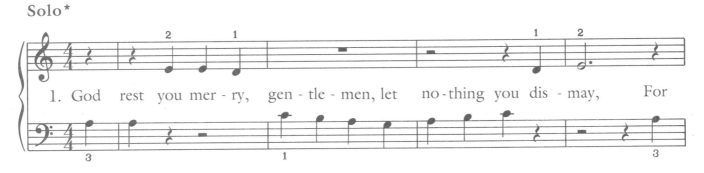

1. God rest you mer - ry, gen - tle - men, let no-thing you dis - may, For

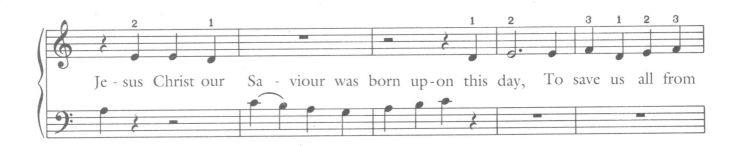

Je - sus Christ our Sa - viour was born up-on this day, To save us all from

Sa - tan's power when we were gone a - stray: O__ ti - dings of com - fort and

joy, com - fort and joy, O__ ti - dings of com - fort and joy.

*To be played 1 octave higher if accompaniment is used.

In the bleak mid-winter

Gustav Holst (1874–1934)

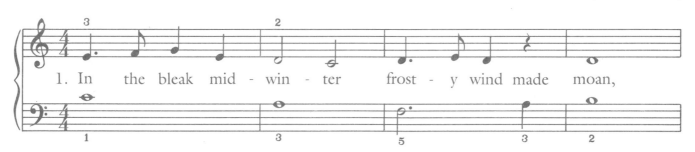

1. In the bleak mid - win - ter frost - y wind made moan,

Earth stood hard as i - ron, wa - ter like a stone;

Snow had fal - len, snow on snow, snow ___ on ___ snow,

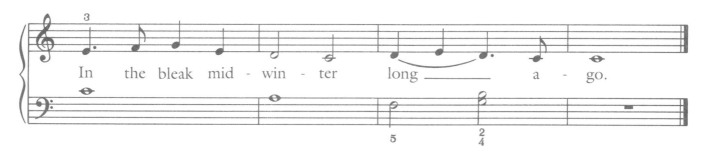

In the bleak mid - win - ter long ___ a - go.

2 Our God, Heav'n cannot hold him
    Nor earth sustain;
  Heav'n and earth shall flee away
    When he comes to reign:
  In the bleak mid-winter
    A stable-place sufficed
  The Lord God Almighty
    Jesus Christ.

3 What can I give him,
    Poor as I am?
  If I were a shepherd
    I would bring a lamb,
  If I were a Wise Man
    I would do my part, —
  Yet what I can I give him,
    Give my heart.

C. Rossetti (1830–94)

The holly and the ivy

English traditional carol

1. The hol-ly and the i-vy when they are both full grown; Of __

all the trees that are in the wood the __ hol-ly bears the crown. The

ri-sing of the sun __ and the run-ning of the deer, The __

play-ing of the mer-ry or-gan, sweet sing-ing in the choir.

2 The holly bears a blossom
   As white as any flower;
   And Mary bore sweet Jesus Christ
   To be our sweet Saviour.
   The rising of the sun (etc.)

3 The holly bears a prickle
   As sharp as any thorn;
   And Mary bore sweet Jesus Christ
   On Christmas Day in the morn.
   The rising of the sun (etc.)

A merry Christmas

Optional accompaniment

A merry Christmas

English traditional carol

Solo*

We wish you a mer-ry Christ-mas, We wish you a mer-ry Christ-mas, We

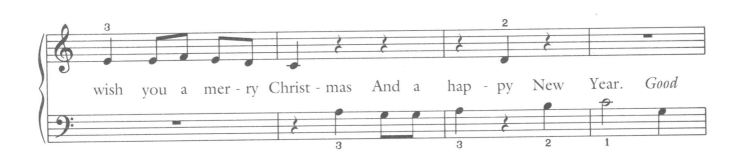

wish you a mer-ry Christ-mas And a hap-py New Year. *Good*

ti - dings we bring To you and your kin; We

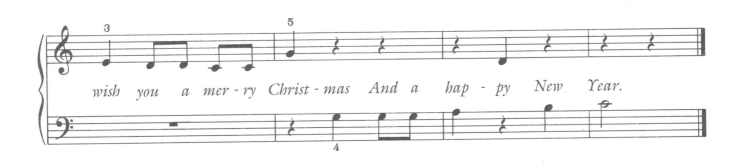

wish you a mer-ry Christ-mas And a hap-py New Year.

*To be played 1 octave higher if accompaniment is used.

21

Jingle, bells

Optional accompaniment

Jingle, bells

Words and melody by J. Pierpont (1822–93)

Solo*

Dash-ing through the snow in a one - horse o - pen sleigh, O - ver fields we

go, laugh-ing all the way; Bells on Bob-tail ring, mak-ing spi - rits

bright; What fun it is to ride, and sing a sleigh - ing song to - night!

Jin - gle, bells, jin - gle, bells, Jin - gle all the way; Oh, what fun it

is to ride in a one - horse o - pen sleigh! Oh, one - horse o - pen sleigh!

*To be played 1 octave higher if accompaniment is used.

Hark! the herald-angels sing

Optional accompaniment

2 Christ, by highest heav'n adored,
Christ, the everlasting Lord,
Late in time behold him come,
Offspring of a virgin's womb!
Veiled in flesh the Godhead see,
Hail th'incarnate Deity,
Pleased as Man with man to dwell,
Jesus, our Emmanuel!
Hark! the herald-angels sing
Glory to the new-born King.

3 Hail the heav'n-born Prince of Peace!
Hail the Sun of Righteousness!
Light and life to all he brings,
Ris'n with healing in his wings;
Mild he lays his glory by,
Born that man no more may die,
Born to raise the sons of earth,
Born to give them second birth.
Hark! the herald-angels sing
Glory to the new-born King.

Charles Wesley (1707–88) and others

Hark! the herald-angels sing

F. Mendelssohn (1809–47)

Solo*

1. Hark! the he - rald - an - gels sing__ Glo - ry to the new-born King; Peace on earth and

mer-cy mild,__ God and sin - ners re - con-ciled: Joy - ful all ye na-tions rise,__

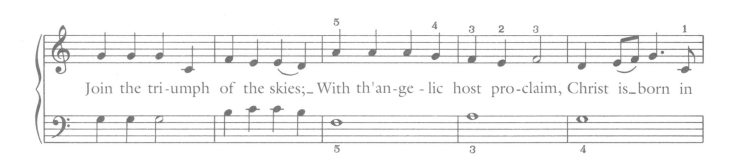

Join the tri-umph of the skies;__ With th'an-ge-lic host pro-claim, Christ is__born in

Beth - le -hem. *Hark! the he - rald an - gels sing Glo - ry__ to the new-born King.*

*To be played 1 octave higher if accompaniment is used.

Ding dong! merrily on high

16th-century French melody

Solo

1. Ding dong! mer - ri - ly on   high   in   heav'n the bells are   ring - ing:
   Ding dong! ve - ri - ly the   sky   is   riv'n with an - gels sing - ing.

Glo -

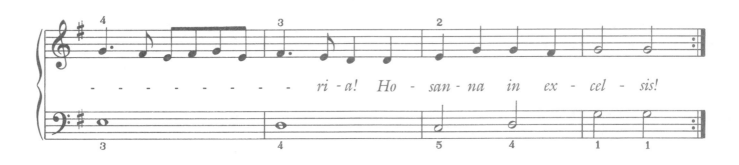

- - - - - - - - - - *ri - a! Ho - san - na in ex - cel - sis!*

26

Ding Dong! merrily on high

Accompaniment

2 E'en so here below, below,
     Let steeple bells be swungen,
  And *i-o, i-o, i-o,*
     By priest and people sungen.
       Gloria! Hosanna in excelsis!

3 Pray you, dutifully prime
     Your matin chime, ye ringers;
  May you beautifully rime
     Your evetime song, ye singers.
       Gloria! Hosanna in excelsis!

G. R. Woodward (1848–1934)

O little town of Bethlehem

English traditional carol
coll. and arr. by R. Vaughan Williams

1. O lit - tle town of Beth - le - hem, how still we — see thee lie! A -

- bove thy deep and dream - less — sleep the si - lent — stars go by. Yet —

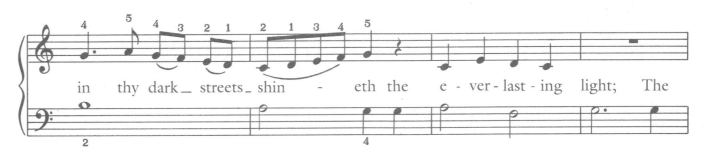

in thy dark — streets — shin - eth the e - ver - last - ing light; The

hopes and fears of all — the — years are met in — thee to - night.

2　O morning stars, together
　　Proclaim the holy birth,
　　And praises sing to God the King,
　　And peace to men on earth;
　　For Christ is born of Mary;
　　And, gathered all above,
　　While mortals sleep, the angels keep
　　Their watch of wondering love.

P. Brooks (1835–93)

Reproduced and printed by Halstan & Co. Ltd., Amersham, Bucks., England